CINDERELLA

A Picture Book

W. H. THWAITE

[ZHINGOORA BOOKS]

This digital edition is published by
Zhingoora Books.

The Cover is Designed by Pallav Sethiya.

zhingoora_books@yahoo.com

CINDERELLA;

HERE once lived a gentleman and his wife, who were the parents of a lovely little daughter.

When this child was only nine years of age, her mother fell sick. Finding her death coming on, she called her child to her and said to her, "My child, always be good; bear every thing that happens to you with patience, and whatever evil and troubles you may suffer, you will be happy in the end if you are so." Then the poor lady died, and her daughter was full of great grief at the loss of a mother so good and kind.

The father too was unhappy, but he sought to get rid of his sorrow by marrying another wife, and he looked out for some prudent lady who might be a second mother to his child, and a companion to himself. His choice fell on a widow lady, of a proud and tyrannical temper, who had two daughters by a former marriage, both as haughty and bad-tempered as their mother. No sooner was the wedding over, than the step-mother began to show her bad temper. She could not bear her step-daughter's good qualities, that only showed up her daughters' unamiable ones still more obviously, and she accordingly compelled the poor girl to do all the drudgery of the household. It was she who washed the dishes, and scrubbed down the stairs, and polished the floors in my lady's chamber and in those of the two pert misses, her daughters; and while the latter slept on good feather beds in elegant rooms, furnished with full-length looking-glasses, their sister

3

lay in a wretched garret on an old straw mattress. Yet the poor thing bore this ill treatment very meekly, and did not dare complain to her father, who thought so much of his wife that he would only have scolded her.

When her work was done, she used to sit in the chimney-corner amongst the cinders, which had caused the nickname of *Cinderella* to be given her by the family; yet, for all her shabby clothes, Cinderella was a hundred times prettier than her sisters, let them be dressed ever so magnificently.

The poor little Cinder-wench! this harsh stepmother was a sore trial to her; and how often, as she sate sadly by herself, did she feel that there is no mother like our own, the dear parent whose flesh and blood we are, and who bears all our little cares and sorrows tenderly as in the apple of her eye!

It happened that the king's son gave a ball, to which he invited all the nobility; and, as our two young ladies made a great figure in the world, they were included in the list of invitations. So they began to be very busy choosing what head-dress and which gown would be the most becoming. Here was fresh work for poor Cinderella: for it was she, forsooth, who was to starch and get up their ruffles, and iron all their fine linen; and nothing but dress was talked about for days together. "I," said the eldest, "shall put on my red velvet dress, with my point-lace trimmings." "And I," said the younger sister, "shall wear my usual petticoat, but shall set it off with my gold brocaded train and my circlet of diamonds."

CINDERELLA DRESSING HER SISTER'S HAIR.

They sent for a clever tire-woman to prepare the double rows of quilling for their caps, and they purchased a quantity of fashionably cut patches. They called in Cinderella to take her advice, as she had such good taste, and Cinderella not only advised them well, but offered to dress their hair, which they were pleased to accept. While she was thus busied, the sisters said to her: "And pray, Cinderella, would you like to go to the ball?"

"Nay, you are mocking me," replied the poor girl; "it is not for such as I to go to balls." "True enough," rejoined they; "folks would laugh to see a Cinderella at a court ball."

These two step-sisters were very cruel to Cinderella, and ill-used her much. Ah! what sweet friends are our own born sisters!—there can be no substitutes like them in the whole wide world.

Any other but Cinderella would have dressed their hair awry to punish them for their impertinence, but she was so good-natured that she dressed them most becomingly. Although they disdained her, and while they would themselves make a great figure in the world, sought to degrade and lower her, see how the lovely disposition of Cinderella shines out. Although she was not allowed to go to the ball of the king's son, she not only advised them well how they could array themselves to appear to the best advantage, but she even— what greatness of heart to do that!—with her own hands dresses their hair, and in the most becoming manner her delicate taste can suggest.

The two sisters were so delighted, that they scarcely ate a morsel for a couple of days. They spent their whole time before a looking-glass, and they would be laced so tight, to make their waists as slender as possible, that more than a dozen stay-laces were broken in the attempt.

The long-wished-for evening came at last, and these proud misses stepped into the carriage and drove away to the palace. Cinderella looked after the coach as far as she could see, and then returned to the kitchen in tears; where, for the first time, she bewailed her hard and cruel degradation. She continued sobbing in the corner of the chimney, until a rapping at the kitchen-door roused her, and she got up to see what had occasioned, it. She found a little old beggar-woman hobbling on crutches, who besought her to give her some food. "I have only part of my own supper for you, Goody, which is no better than a dry crust. But if you like to step in and warm yourself, you can do so, and welcome." "Thank you, my dear," said the old woman in a feeble, croaking voice. She then hobbled in and took her seat by the fire.

"Hey! dearee me! what are all these tears, my child?" said the old woman. And then Cinderella told the old woman all her griefs; how her sisters had gone to the ball, and how she wished to go too, but had no clothes, or means to do so.

"But you *shall* go, my darling," said the old woman, "or I am not Queen of the Faëries or your Godmother. Dry up your tears like a good god-daughter and do as I bid you, and you shall have clothes and horses finer than any one."

Cinderella had heard her father often talk of her godmother, and tell her that she was one of those good faëries who protect children. Her spirits revived, and she wiped away her tears.

The faëry took Cinderella by the hand, and said, "Now, my dear, go into the garden and fetch me a pumpkin." Cinderella bounded lightly to execute her commands, and returned with one of the finest and largest pumpkins she could meet with. It was as big as a beer barrel, and Cinderella trundled it into the kitchen, wondering what her godmother would do with it. Her godmother took the pumpkin, and scooped out the inside of it, leaving nothing but rind; she then struck it with her wand, and it instantly became one of the most elegant gilt carriages ever seen.

She next sent Cinderella into the pantry for the mouse-trap, bidding her bring six little mice alive which she would find in the trap. Cinderella hastened to the pantry, and there found the mice as the faëry had said, which she brought to the old lady, who told her to lift up the door of the trap but a little way and very gently, so that only one of the mice might go out at a time.

Cinderella raised the mouse-trap door, and as the mice came out one by one, the old woman touched them with her wand, and transformed them into fine prancing dapple-gray carriage horses with long manes and tails, which were tied up with light-blue ribands.

"Now, my dear good child," said the faëry, "here you have a coach and horses, much handsomer than your sisters', to say the least of them; but as we have neither a postilion nor a coachman to take care of them, run quickly to the stable, where the rat-trap is placed, and bring it to me."

Cinderella was full of joy, and did not lose a moment; and soon returned with the trap, in which there were two fine large rats. These, too, were touched with the wand, and immediately the one was changed into a smart postilion, and the other into a jolly-looking coachman in full finery.

Her godmother then said, "My dear Cinderella, you must go to the garden again before I can complete your equipage; when you get there, keep to the right side, and close to the wall you will see the watering-pot standing; look behind it, and there you will find six lizards, which you must bring to me immediately."

Cinderella hastened to the garden as she was desired, and found the six lizards, which she put into her apron and brought to the faëry. Another touch of the wonderful wand soon converted them into six spruce footmen in dashing liveries, with powdered hair and pig-tails, three-cornered cocked hats and gold-headed canes, who immediately jumped up behind the carriage as nimbly as if they had been footmen and nothing else all their lives.

The coachman and postilion having likewise taken their places, the faëry said to Cinderella, "Well, my dear girl, is not this as fine an equipage as you could desire to go to the ball with? Tell me, now, are you pleased with it?"

"O yes, dear godmother," replied Cinderella; and then, with a good deal of hesitation, added, "but how can I make my appearance among so many finely-dressed people in these mean-looking clothes?"

"Give yourself no uneasiness about that, my dear; the most laborious part of our task is already accomplished, and it will be hard if I cannot make your dress correspond with your coach and servants."

On saying this, the old woman, assuming her character of Queen of the Faëries, touched Cinderella with the magic wand, and her clothes were instantly changed into a most magnificent ball dress, ornamented with the most costly jewels. The faëry took from her pocket a beautiful pair of elastic glass slippers, which she caused Cinderella to put on, and then desired her to get into the carriage with all expedition, as the ball had already commenced.

Two footmen opened the carriage door, and assisted the now beautifully dressed Cinderella into it. Her godmother, before she took leave, strictly charged her, on no account whatever to stay at the ball after the clock had struck twelve; and then added, that if she stopped but a single moment beyond that time, her fine coach, horses, coachman, postilion, and footmen, and fine apparel, would all return to their original shapes of pumpkin, mice, rats, lizards, and mean-looking clothes.

Cinderella promised faithfully to attend to every thing that the faëry had mentioned; and then, quite overjoyed, gave the direction to the footman, who bawled out in a loud and commanding tone to the coachman, "To the Royal Palace." The coachman touched his prancing horses lightly with his whip, and swiftly the carriage started off, and in a short time reached the palace.

CINDERELLA'S ARRIVAL AT THE PALACE IN HER ELEGANT GILT CARRIAGE, WHICH ATTRACTS GENERAL NOTICE AS IT DRIVES UP TO THE MARBLE PORTICO; OF WHICH INFORMATION IS COMMUNICATED TO THE PRINCE, WHO HASTENS TO THE DOOR AND WELCOMES CINDERELLA, HANDS HER OUT OF THE CARRIAGE, AND GRACEFULLY LEADS HER INTO THE PALACE, WHERE THE NOBLES WELCOME HER AS A PRINCESS.

The arrival of so splendid an equipage as Cinderella's could not fail to attract general notice at the palace gates; and as it drove up to the marble portico, the servants in great numbers came out to see it. Information was quickly taken to the king's son, that a beautiful young lady, evidently some princess, was in waiting. His Royal Highness hastened to the door, welcomed Cinderella, and handed her out of the carriage. He then led her gracefully into the ball-room, and introduced her to his father, the king. The moment she appeared, all conversation was hushed, the violins ceased playing, and the dancing stopped short, so great was the sensation produced by the stranger's beauty. A confused murmur of admiration fluttered through the crowd, and each was fain to exclaim, "How surpassingly lovely she is!" The ladies were all busy examining her head-dress and her clothes, in order to get similar ones the very next day, if, indeed, they could meet with stuffs of such rich patterns, and find workwomen clever enough to make them up. "What a lovely creature! so fair!— so beautiful!—What a handsome figure!—how elegantly she is dressed!" Even the prince's father, old as he was, could not behold her with indifference, but wiped his eye-glass and used it very much, and said very often to the queen, that he had never seen so sweet a being.

CINDERELLA IS PRESENTED BY THE PRINCE TO THE KING AND QUEEN, WHO WELCOME HER WITH THE HONORS DUE TO A GREAT PRINCESS, AND IS THEN LED INTO THE ROYAL BALL-ROOM.

The king's son handed Cinderella to one of the most distinguished seats on the daïs at the top of the Hall, and begged she would allow him to hand her some refreshments. Cinderella received them with great grace. When this was over, the prince requested to have the honour of dancing with her. Cinderella smiled consent; and the delighted prince immediately led her out to the head of the dance, just about to commence. The eyes of the whole company were fixed upon the beautiful pair.

The trumpets sounded and the music struck up, and the dance commenced; but if Cinderella's beauty, elegant figure, and the splendor of her dress, had before drawn the attention of the whole room, the astonishment at her dancing was still greater.

Gracefulness seemed to play in all her motions; the airy lightness with which she floated along—as buoyant as thistle-down—drew forth a general murmur of admiration. The hall rang with the loudest acclamations of applause, and the company, all in one voice, pronounced her the most elegant creature that had ever been seen. And this was the little girl who had passed a great part of her life in the kitchen, and had always been called a "Cinder-wench."

When the dance was ended, a magnificent feast was served up, consisting of all delicacies: so much was the young prince engaged with Cinderella, that he did not eat one morsel of the supper.

Cinderella drew near her sisters, and frequently spoke to them; and in her goodness of heart she offered them the delicacies which she had received from the prince: but they did not know she was their sister.

When Cinderella heard the clock strike three-quarters past eleven, she made a low courtesy to the whole assembly and retired in haste.

You see how fortune befriends the good-hearted, and even out of such unpromising material as a pumpkin and mice, can make a coach and six, with which to honor her worthy favorite. So Cinderella goes to the ball; but to teach her to be diligent and faithful in her engagements, her faëry godmother enjoins upon her that she return home at twelve. Native beauty and grace attract the princely heart; and while the king's son pays no heed to her pretentious sisters, he is all grace and condescension to little Cinderella. Obedient to her engagement with her godmother, she returns in all the splendor and honor of the coach and six.

On reaching home, she found her godmother; and after thanking her for the treat she had enjoyed, she ventured to express a wish to return to the ball on the following evening, as the prince had requested her to do.

She was still relating to her godmother all that had happened at court, when her two sisters knocked at the door. Cinderella went and let them in, pretending to yawn and stretch herself, and rub her eyes, and saying, "How late you are!" just as if she was waked up out of a nap, though, truth to say, she had never felt less disposed to sleep in her life. "If you had been to the ball," said one of the sisters, "you would not have thought it late. There came the most beautiful princess ever seen, who loaded us with polite attentions, and gave us oranges and citrons."

Cinderella could scarcely contain her delight, and inquired the name of the princess. But they replied that nobody knew her name, and that the king's son was in great trouble about her, and would give the world to know who she could be. "Is she, then, so very beautiful?" said Cinderella, smiling. "Oh, my! how I should like to see her! Oh, do, my Lady Javotte, lend me the yellow dress you wear every day, that I may go to the ball and have a peep at this wonderful princess." "A likely story, indeed!" cried Javotte, tossing her head disdainfully, "that I should lend my clothes to a dirty Cinderella like you!"

Cinderella expected to be refused, and was not sorry for it, as she would have been puzzled what to do, had her sister really lent her the dress she begged to have.

On the following evening the sisters again went to the court ball, and so did Cinderella, dressed even more magnificently than before. The king's son never left her side, and kept paying her the most flattering attentions. The young lady was nothing loth to listen to him; so it came to pass that she forgot her godmother's injunctions, and, indeed, lost her reckoning so completely, that before she deemed it could be eleven o'clock, she was startled at hearing the first stroke of midnight. She rose hastily, and flew away like a startled fawn. The prince attempted to follow her, but she was too swift for him; only, as she flew she dropped one of her glass slippers, which he picked up very eagerly. Cinderella reached home quite out of breath, without either coach or footmen, and with only her shabby clothes on her back; nothing, in short, remained of her recent magnificence, save a little glass slipper, the fellow to the one she had lost.

CINDERELLA DANCING WITH THE PRINCE IS ADMIRED FOR HER GRACEFULNESS. THE CLOCK STRIKES TWELVE: SHE HAVING FORGOT HER GOD-MOTHER'S INSTRUCTIONS, IS ALARMED, FLIES OUT OF THE BALL-ROOM--HER GORGEOUS APPAREL IS CHANGED INTO THE DRESS OF A CINDER-WENCH, AND HER SPLENDID EQUIPAGE INTO A PUMPKIN, RATS, MICE AND LIZARDS.

The sentinels at the palace gate were closely questioned as to whether they had not seen a princess coming out; but they answered they had seen no one except a shabbily dressed girl, who appeared to be a peasant rather than a young lady.

On this second night, as you have taken notice, dazzled by worldly show and the pleasing flattery of her royal lover, Cinderella over-stays her time, and is compelled to make her way back to her father's house on foot and in rags—an everlasting lesson to all the pretty little Cinderellas in the world to keep their word, and to act in good faith by such as befriend them. Never mind—her heart is in the right place— she is a charming good creature; and although virtue goes home in rags, it will leave some token behind—some foot-print by which it can be known and traced wherever it has once walked. We shall hear from that little lost glass slipper again!

CINDERELLA RETURNED SHABBILY DRESSED.

When the two sisters returned from the ball, Cinderella asked them whether they had been well entertained; and whether the beautiful lady was there? They replied, that she was; but that she had run away as soon as midnight had struck, and so quickly as to drop one of her dainty glass slippers, which the king's son had picked up, and was looking at most fondly during the remainder of the ball; indeed, it seemed beyond a doubt that he was deeply enamored of the beautiful creature to whom it belonged.

They spoke truly enough; for, a few days afterwards, the king's son caused a proclamation to be made, by sound of trumpet all over the kingdom, to the effect that he would marry her whose foot should be found to fit the slipper exactly. So the slipper was first tried on by all the princesses; then by all the duchesses; and next by all the persons belonging to the court; but in vain. It was then carried to the two sisters, who tried with all their might to force their feet into its delicate proportions, but with no better success. Cinderella, who was present, and recognized her slipper, now laughed, and said, "Suppose I were to try?" Her sisters ridiculed such an idea; but the gentleman who was appointed to try the slipper, having looked attentively at Cinderella, and perceived how beautiful she was, said that it was but fair she should do so, as he had orders to try it on every young maiden in the kingdom. Accordingly, having requested Cinderella to sit down, she no sooner put her little foot to the slipper, than she drew it on, and it fitted like wax. The sisters were quite amazed; but their astonishment increased tenfold when Cinderella drew the fellow slipper out of her pocket, and put it on. Her godmother then made her appearance; and, having touched Cinderella's clothes with her wand, made them still more magnificent than those she had previously worn.

THE HERALDS OF THE COURT ANNOUNCE THE PROCLAMATION THAT THE PRINCE WOULD MARRY THE LADY WHOM THE GLASS SLIPPER FITTED. CINDERELLA TRIES ON THE SLIPPER, WHICH FITS HER DELICATE FOOT, TO THE GREAT ASTONISHMENT OF HER FAMILY.

Her two sisters now recognized her for the beautiful stranger they had seen at the ball; and, falling at her feet, implored her forgiveness for their unworthy treatment, and all the insults they had heaped upon her head. Cinderella raised them, saying, as she embraced them, that she not only forgave them with all her heart, but wished for their affection. She was then taken to the palace of the young prince, in whose eyes she appeared yet more lovely than before, and who married her shortly after.

Cinderella, who was as good as she was beautiful, allowed her sisters to lodge in the palace, and gave them in marriage, that same day, to two lords belonging to the court.

MARRIAGE OF THE PRINCE AND CINDERELLA.

The amiable qualities of Cinderella were as conspicuous after as they had been before marriage.

End of the book.

www.ingramcontent.com/pod-product-compliance
Lightning Source LLC
Chambersburg PA
CBHW060022300526

45794CB00003B/1263